GENERAL DISCHARGE

Poems

Gary Mesick

Fomite

Burlington, VT

ISBN-13: 978-1-944388-82-9
Library of Congress Control Number: 2018967927
Fomite
58 Peru Street

Burlington, VT 05401

To every American taxpayer: You're welcome.

And as for war, my wars
Were global from the start.
—Henry Reed, "Unarmed Combat"

TABLE OF CONTENTS

ACKNOWLEDGEMENTS

Some of the poems in this book first appeared elsewhere, as indicated below:

Alimentum: The Literature of Food: "Cooking Show"

Café Review: "To My Track Driver, On Trial," "Attack of the Blue Tarp Zombies," and "The Man in Flames"

Caveat Lector: "Wasps"

Confrontation: "Smoker"

Grasslimb: "Speed Trap at the North Fort Gate," "Road Crew Babe," and "Lunch Hour at *Pho* Saigon"

Main Street Rag: "War Games"

North American Review: "The Anti-War Movement, 1974"

New American Writing: "Great Books of the Western World"

Parody: "Crab Lice"

Sugar House Review: "The GI Handbook: Travel Tip #42"

TAB: A Journal of Poetry and Poetics: "Compline: Camp Casey," and "It Wasn't the War"

Of Arms and the Man

The Anti-War Movement, 1974

Armored Personnel Carriers sat un-Guarded
De-facing our school, so, having no greater cause
To occupy our time, we found several sticks of chalk
That would not be missed and went to work.

Somewhere else, the earnest caretakers of the APCs
Hand-to-handed out leaflets and declared the virtues of service
In the National Guard. Meanwhile, we crept, concealed by junipers
And rhododendrons to the edge of the garden,
Then darted between the two parked, tracked vehicles,
Until we reached the far flank. Then with our chalk,
We traced encircled semaphores for peace,
And we exhorted no one in particular to Stop the War,
Which was, to all reasonable persons, already defunct.

Nobody prevented us nor cheered us on,
And our handiwork was surely gone with the first good rain,
Of which there was plenty in Seattle between that November
And the day I entered West Point the following July.

Pascal's Wager: The Cold War Edition

I had long since lost my faith in institutions,
From the President of the United
States to the Chappaquiddick Water Safety
Commission. The Revolution was stalled out,
And the redistribution of wealth, postponed.

I was too short to play forward, and my
Jump shot lost inertia outside the free
Throw lane. Tuition aid to a boy with
No vertical leap came in uniform.

I resigned myself to mutually assured
Destruction, and I would die in my footsteps
With feet clad in combat boots or sandals.
But surely we were tired after a generation
Of saving a people from itself. No more
Nation building—at least for a time.

And until then, in my Dress Gray
Or olive drab ghetto, I could still read
Rolling Stone. I could even sport my Moscow
State University tee-shirt—during
Authorized study hours or weekend passes.

And all the while I would will myself to
Believe that rationality might still
Hold sway—and that hair brushing the tips
Of my ears was a bold act of defiance.

THE MAN IN THE RED SASH

"You will report to him first. When he says
'Drop your bags,' do exactly as you're told,"
he said, and I nodded. "If you don't," he
warned, "he'll tell you to pick them up, then drop
your bags again." *How clever*, I thought, *that
West Point presents its first lesson in unconditional
obedience wrapped in word-play. And how clever I am
to know in advance exactly what to do.*

I thanked my informant and
packed my bag carefully for my
encounter with The Man
in the Red Sash, wrapping my every
possession—alarm clock, spit-polished
shoes, soap, razor, shaving cream, stamps, stationery,
and pocket guide to New York City—in tee shirts, briefs
and socks. That weekend, I practiced dropping it from
heights and satisfied myself the locks would hold.

When, at seventeen, I arrived on the other
side of the continent, I saw with satisfaction
that the scene was just as advertised, and I took
my place in line. I watched the boy
in front of me approach
and set his suitcase gently
at his side, so as not to break
his alarm clock or scratch his polished
shoes, then lift it up, again,

and again, and again. And I was secretly
pleased at his misfortune, sniggering
quietly as I waited to confront and confound
The Man in the Red Sash.

My turn arrived, and I sprang
forward. He said, "Drop," and I surrendered
my bag to gravity while his eyes widened
in surprise. For that one instant, he had
nothing to say, and I basked in my success until
my triumphant moment receded into the past. Then both
The Man in the Red Sash and I recognized
in my singular achievement the exhaustion
of my knowledge of West Point, of obedience, of
discipline, and together we surveyed the
wasteland of my future, for which I had not seen
the script, stretched out before me.

FILMING *MACARTHUR* ON LOCATION AT WEST POINT
WITH MY OLD FRIEND GREGORY PECK

I suppose you could call it a speaking part,

Although it wasn't a line, exactly—

Rather, more of an utterance,

A spontaneous release of surprise and amusement,

Coated in a warmth that served to say,

"Yes, we are members of the same club, you and I."

I practiced all morning

With two thousand of my peers.

Meanwhile, the professional

Wrung the nuance from his quip

As they shot him, first from one side,

Then the other,

Then from far away,

Then in tight focus,

Then peering over his shoulder at all of us until,

After the thirtieth take, we became old friends—

His joke, my laugh—

Any edge long worn away, like river rock,

The moment transmuted

Into a courteous grunt of acknowledgment

Toward something we knew

Wasn't all that funny to begin with.

In the end, it was watchable,

And I screened it occasionally,

Listening for my voice in the chorus,

Pointing out to others

The place where I would have been,

If not on the cutting room floor,

Having played my part in building

Perhaps not the monument, but the scaffolding.

Last Class with Balls

In cowardice, I joined the Infantry.
West Point does not imbue its graduates
With "Duty, Honor, Country" and confer
Commissions with the expectation of
A life of service to the nation as
The O-Club Manager at Heidelberg,
You know. The year before, when (rumor was)
Some Pointer—following the rules, mind you—
Selected leading barmaids as his post,
The indignation resonated from
The Hudson River to the Pentagon.
And still, I lusted after such a gig
Within the Adjutant General's Corps.
My job: to oversee some Hofbrauhaus,
Where the Saint Pauli Girl herself would stride
Across the broad plank floor to tender beer
Steins, slopping foam against her ample breasts,
To regiments of Cold War cavalry
Returned from border duty, hostages
To some unlikely cataclysm miles
Away. If pressed, I might have been convinced
To undertake some more respectable
Pursuit. Perhaps the Corps of Engineers
Could find a waterway sufficiently
Secluded to remove me from harm's way.
The Signal Corps had air-conditioned vans
To house their delicate machines. Although
I might still die, I wouldn't have to break

A sweat. Intelligence, or Ordnance Corps,
Or Transportation, Finance—any one
Would do. An Army needs them all. While cooks,
Mechanics, and truck drivers may not seem
Too sexy, try to fight a war without
Them. Privately, we joked, "Why walk when you
Can ride? Why ride when you can hide?" But trust
The institution to arrange for a
More public measure of our mettle and
Collective manhood. So, as members of
The last all-male class, the so-called Last Class
With Balls, we had to rise and, one by one,
In front of the assemblage, to announce
Our billet to the world. And when the crowd
Had duly noted each selection with
Derision or applause, each young man sat
To ponder the new terrors that his choice
Had wrought. When at last having heard my name,
I stood, and for the sake of nothing but
The satisfaction manifested in
A murmur from the room, forsook the air-
Conditioned vans and foamy pilsners, and,
The coward that I was, became a grunt.

Soldier of Fortune

The war's end began his misfortune.
Born too late to fight the last one
He feared he would never see another.
Without an enemy in his sights, he served
Without purpose, trained without conviction
And found it tedious.

Once free of his commission and his oath
He moved to the sound of the guns,
Not particular about the theater or the cause.

Of course, the shrapnel that tore through
His organs played no favorites either.

At seventeen, as plebes, he and I had reached
The same erroneous conclusion. Had we foreseen
How easily war finds a way, it might
Have saved his life. I, on the other hand,
May have found somewhat less consolation.

It Wasn't the War

It wasn't the war that terrified me
But that late Saturday night when I was alone,
Only weeks from turning twenty-three,
A loaded forty-five holstered at one hip
And a walkie-talkie swaying from the other.
I descended the grimy basement stairwell
And stepped into the dark hall of the Enlisted Club,
Grateful for the baggy fatigues
To hide the tremors in my knees.

And there I stood, the Officer of the Day,
Facing sixty men, scarred from battle
And the tattoo needle, men our country paid
And trained to kill, men who believed in little
Except that they had time for another beer
Or two, men who glanced at me with mild amusement
As I croaked, "Closing time, Gentlemen."

To my Track Driver, on Trial

What can I say that would help you now?

That I had no right to my amused surprise
When you saw your first sheep and mistook them
For a breed of unusually hirsute cattle,
Since you had only seen bull terriers for reference?

That, though I loathed spending the night with you
Pulling and replacing our drive train, and I berated you
For not challenging the order that sent us plunging
Into the ravine under that moonless sky,
I was secretly flattered (being barely old enough to drink myself)
That you would drive off a cliff
On just my say-so?

That you were fiercely loyal to me.
That the other guy wasn't half the soldier
You should have been. That you were a straight arrow
When sober. That you were bound for jail
Before you were born. That your doom is insufferable,
Like cancer. And that I can only hope you captured
Some remembered joy in those few allotted years you had
Before stabbing your bunkmate over that half-empty bottle
Of Olde English 800.

SMOKER

When all the uppercuts and roundhouse hooks

And jabs propelled in anger one grudge match

Upon another are exhausted, and

Two pair of unclaimed padded gloves lie in

The sand, a medic tends to cuts with swabs

And rubbing alcohol. Blood and sweat stain

The battle dress of those who fought before.

Behind them, rifles stacked in teepees rest,

And Humvees parked in columns point toward

The border just eleven clicks away,

Awaiting orders. Other men remain,

Reluctant to depart just yet. Behind

Them, captains loiter, studying their men,

And talk among themselves, not offering

Direction. This show is NCO work.

And then the crowd howls as one man steps up

To lift a pair of empty gloves up from

The ground and, smirking, he dares anyone

To do the same. The chests of those too big

Or small relax. And meanwhile the right-sized

Unwilling try to melt away. At last

The awkward silence ends when someone shouts

A name, but no one answers him until

Another soldier shoves the man in front

Of him into the circle, where The Whole

Elects him with its acclamation and

The ring around him closes, eager for

The clash of glove on skull. The crowd appoints
His second, who will lace his gloves and tend
His wounds between each round. Then, gingerly
He hops about and tentatively takes
Some punches at the air. He hears a voice
Shout "Fight!" and starts to circle, with no cause
To hit this man, or reason to be hit,
Except the ring is here, and watching him,
And it has anyhow become his turn
To make at least a show of violence
Or be found out before the shooting starts.

RULES OF EVIDENCE

He had just invested his paycheck in those drugs
And he had been loath to flush it all away—
The money, the release, the sense of triumph
Over the small-minded. So he hesitated.

Now they bobbed helplessly in the toilet bowl
While his sergeant fetched the MPs and his
Lieutenant stood fast between him and the trip
Lever, watching him watch his stash
Grow more waterlogged and more useless
Except as an exhibit at his court martial.

War Games

Then, after two long days, we took the hill,
But I had nothing left to give. Afraid
And weary from the fight, I lacked the will
To do my duty, or at least persuade
My men to do as much and stay awake
To guard against the next counterattack.
And four hours later I woke at daybreak
To find a stranger kicking at my back
And boots. I was alone. And I could hear
Him mutter soothingly, but not a sound
Made sense. I shrugged. He smiled. And it was clear
To us that there was nobody around
With means to properly receive the tender
Of my foe's unconditional surrender.

Enhanced Interrogation

The man tucks his leather gloves away.
The prisoner gathers what remains of his clothes and dresses.

"Most say they hope they never see me again."
The man forces a laugh that neither of them believes.

"Oh, no," the prisoner says. "I absolutely *do* hope to see you again!"
Surprised, even pleased, the man nods in affirmation.
"It is because you and I see the world in the same way."

And so the man doesn't see at all,
Doesn't see that the prisoner means nothing
Except that seeing the man means he will have lived.

BREAKER MORANT

It was irresistible, like gravity.
With the Magazine Lee-Enfield, his "Emily,"
A skilled rifleman could squeeze her
Fast enough to bring two dozen Boer
Kommandos to their sticky end
In a mad minute.

Emily was the law of the Velt,
Where rules of expediency
Eclipsed rules of evidence;
Where you didn't ask why, but how;
Where you may as well have asked a dog
Why it licks its hind parts.

High Noon at the DMZ

He wasn't likely to miss at this range,

Only six inches from my brainpan.

I could see my destination from where we stood,

And I was running late. But he was being difficult,

And now we were at an impasse.

I don't know why I imagined

My inability to read a map trumped

His standing orders. But when my pointing

And gesturing failed to win him over

And I motioned for my men to advance,

He pressed the butt of his rifle to his shoulder

To inform me that we were on the same side,

And he aimed to keep it that way.

COMPLINE: CAMP CASEY

There is a monastic order to life
Here, among the relics
Of conflict older than these trees,
Among the vaulted arches
Of corrugated Quonset huts,
Among armed men keeping vigil
Over bridges with pre-chambered charges,
Where retaining walls double as bastions,
And the amber rice lies in open fields
Of fire before them,
Forever and ever
War without end.

Rise, dress, stretch, and run,
Work until I have had my fill,
Then read, write, and think.
The Stars and Stripes is a red,
White, and blue tabloid,
With pictures and box scores
And precious little news;
Letters home, a litany of longings;
Thoughts, more like wishes;
And neither news, nor letters, nor wishes
Can transport me beyond the gates
Of this secular monastery.

Just beyond are those we serve
And those we fear,
And the hell of it is,

We can't tell the difference.

We do our duty,

Killing and dying as infrequently as possible.

We drill and train,

Run and march and ride,

Hugging the misty hillsides,

Fording the pungent rivers,

Avoiding Happy Mountains

(The sacred burial mounds)

Where grass grows lush and full.

They farm rice and ginseng within the range fan,

So we ensure the impact area

Is at least reasonably clear of men

And women before we shoot.

We pay *solatium* to the families

Of those we kill.

Even as taps sounds, tanks rumble

Yards from where I sleep;

A medevac helicopter hovers

Over the aid station—and yet

There is no war.

But this Godforsaken place

Knows no peace,

And poses all the troubling questions

Without offering any hope of definitive answers

(As any self-respecting monastic order would),

Which makes this the worst

Or the best

Of all possible worlds.

YANKEE, GO HOME!

We kept to ourselves.
Between patrols, we withdrew behind
The concertina and the walled fortress,
And by mutual consent, generally confined
Our recreational ventures to the GI ghettos
That are the price of occupation.

Each time I came and went, I passed
The monument at the entrance, streaked with
Orange spray paint. It took weeks
Or months before I recognized it as writing.
A message. But to whom?

I couldn't read the script. Hell,
I rarely ate the food. And so I motored past,
Oblivious, until I finally gave voice
To my curiosity, goading a local into
A reluctant translation, and I was welcomed
Into the long ranks of the Unwelcome.
I knew I had arrived once I understood
They were telling me to leave.

Stand-To

Beauty rests as much in the pause as in the phrase.
I woke not to the cock's crow, but to the in-between silence.
The quiet seemed complete, as if all the world
Had come to an end, except for him and me.
He would crow, pause, and then crow again and again.
Each time, I imagined him gathering
For another outburst of pride, as if every exhale
Lay claim to the world around him:
"Mine! Mine! Mine!"

But then I heard what seemed to be an echo,
Yet not an echo. Rather, an answer. And then,
More faintly still, I heard another. And I understood
The cock had rested not just to inhale, but also to listen
To other claims to other hillsides, and I knew him
Not as soloist but as part of the choir,
Whose entrances were metered to the acoustics of the hillsides.
And their pauses were intricately linked
To give each his voice in this vast chorus as
"Mine" became "Ours."

THE GI HANDBOOK: TRAVEL TIP #42

If you choose to buy a *Vogue* in Paris—
Not to read, but as a souvenir
For the girl you left behind—
Look for an unsympathetic kiosk vendor.

You say *Vogue* as in "rogue;"
He says *Vogue* as in "dog."
The nuance is lost on you, but not on him.
You agree, the difference no difference to your ear,
And affirm the rogue, who insists on the dog,
And back and forth you go until
Either he turns away to receive another's custom
Or you master the open mid-back rounded vowel.

And your lesson in applied phonetics
Will serve you better and more faithfully
Than the magazine,
Or the girl.

Backstage with the Richard Nixon Comeback Tour

A cocktail hour of fetching behind us,
I was superfluous,
And so I sat at a butcher's table
In the kitchen with the other drivers
And aides de camp, complaining of our lot
And waiting, while in the main room,
The grateful leaders of a nation
Gathered near their patroness,
Heiress to a fortune in cabled wire,
As a yet-unregenerate Richard Nixon,
Once captain of them all,
Struck the piano, and led them
In a chorus of "Happy Birthday."

WE COME IN PEACE!

The rotor blades shrieked and the engine
Consumed itself in one last surge
Before the impact buried the skids in mud
And sent our heads rebounding against the hull.

Dizzy, sore, surrounded, outgunned,
We marshalled all our diplomacy and cash
To persuade our captors we didn't care
Who they were, and their fields meant nothing
To us but a welcome piece of wet, flat ground
For our crippled craft to crash.

At last they allowed us to radio for help
Then escorted us a safe distance away
Where they knew by the time help came
And we could make our way back
No one would find any trace
Of their drug operation there, deep
In the Pine Barrens of New Jersey.

lappled light

branch and

ιy like a

ι, glide like a fingernail

ιne spine of this ridgeline, let

ιour backdraft send leaves skipping

Across the pavement, accelerate

Through the curve just to feel the road

Tugging at the wheel, and bless

Those civil engineers who designed

Without limits, as you crest the rise

And reach the bridge between

Weekday and weekend, traveling just

Fast enough that you no longer

Observe, but become, for that brief

Moment, oblivious to the world

In which joy like this deserves

To be punished.

AMBITION

When I retire,

I will be like Raymond Burr.

I'll never use another razor,

And I'll just buy a larger suit

As often as my expanding girth requires.

I'll retreat to Denver,

Or the Napa Valley,

To fail repeatedly at each new venture,

Only coming out of the hills

When I need the attention,

Or the cash,

Unrecognizable to anyone

Who knew me then,

And grousing the entire time

At having to reprise the one role

I was ever born to play.

Thank You for Your Service

Stonehenge at Maryhill, Washington

As statements go, his is a quiet plaint,
A lonely, wind-swept presence
Set between the river and the reservation,
With the cross ties and the columns
Redeployed into a nearly-perfect circle
Of concrete-and-rebar slabs
To manifest one man's lament
Upon the sacrifice of innocents
To the voracious gods
Of our least worthy and most primitive natures.

But archeology has since revealed Sam Hill's error—
And his genius—
The ruddy Slaughter Stone is free of blood,
Just rich in iron; turns out Stonehenge
Didn't need their sacrifices after all,
Any more than Flanders, or The Somme.

THE CENTRALIA MASSACRE, 1919

In Centralia, there isn't much
To speak of: to the west
Of the freeway, an outlet mall sells
Last year's shoes at what must be
Discount prices, and to the east,
Near the antiques mall, where
The old Roderick Hotel had
Stood, you can see where Buffalo
Bill once slept, and where,
Nine years later, Legionnaires
Marched on Armistice Day against
The Wobblies and set the place
On fire. Four of them were
Shot for their trouble, but
They managed to find Wesley
Everett, both Union agitator and
Veteran of the War, on Mellen
Street, and drop him at the bridge,
Dangling from a rope. But no one
Speaks much of that.

The Man in the Gray Flannel Suit

I know five ways to kill you
With my bare hands. Or is it four?
I'm reasonably certain it is five,
But I seem to have misplaced one
In the fog of years. It won't matter,
Because you'll be dead after the first,
Or the second (In addition to memory loss,
I have become less efficient).

I trot this out from time to time for
The smoldering self that shifts, uneasy
Beneath the trimmed lawn, beyond the garaged cars
And the retirement plan. Its recollection
Makes inanities uttered in meetings,
Slights encountered while attempting to merge,
Obsequious sales associates, inattentive waiters,
And intrusive interview questions just a bit more
Bearable, since enduring it all is a choice
And the arsenal of alternatives always
Lie precisely within my reach.

The lessons of war were a passage
Through a portal, where conduct required
Shedding the cloak of civility,
Which, upon my return, I never found again.
And I mourn its loss each time my scarred
Fingers fumble with the necktie at my throat.

Lunch Hour at *Pho* Saigon

A pair of chromed figures, winged and bearded,
The size of mastiffs—but rather small for dragons—
Crouch beside the doors to this converted
Filling station, extending their exotic,
And misapprehended brand of luck
And protection to the mid-day diners at *Pho* Saigon.
Saigon! As if the name itself is gesture enough
To will the customers into blissful defiance of the past.

Lunch is politics by other means.
To the man on a tight schedule, propped against the counter
While taking phone calls between the mouthfuls
Of the translucent noodles, his noon meal has no agenda
Beyond efficiency: it's cheap and it's quick.

He breathes in this air, rich with the scent of lemon,
Ginger, anise, and cardamom, cinnamon,
Mint, coriander and *nuoc mam*. And so the wisdom
Of generations is devoured without a care.

It seems so easy—until the pepper sauce,
Or the collapse of a marionette regime,
Or the hand-lettered sign above the doorway
Causes one to rediscover the eternal verity:
You must always pay as you leave.
And the dragons' ambiguous gaze
Is an unsettling reminder that one man's angel
Is another's demon.

LLOYD'S ROCKET

The low-slung cantilever roofline
Still slices rakishly across the face
Of the double-bay garage at Lloyd's Rocket
Like a snap-brim iron fedora.
Here, once, Lloyd and pimply
Teenage attendants in overalls dispensed dreams
Of reaching the Infinite for eight dollars a tankful
Beneath a bright red steel-plate phallus.
And we knew with each purchase,
We took dead aim at the stars
And the Russkies. In comparison, real lunar landings
Made for an inferior spectacle.
We soon grew bored and, as it always will,
Euphoria dissipated into commonplace.
In time even our Enemy
Crumpled like a paper tiger, with Fear Itself
Displaced by the dull ache of a purpose
Forsaken in its fulfillment.
But even now, in its abandoned state,
Faded to pink and teetering from its rusted pole,
Lloyd's Rocket rises above the chain-link fence,
Still reaches upwards for a once-impalpable moon
And the unbounded hope we found in a full tank of gas
That could take us anywhere but here.

RESUME

I see here that you've served overseas.
Led a platoon. That's what?—Five?
No, thirty—men. And a company. I
Assume that's bigger. With twenty-four-hour
Charge of their performance,
Their behavior, their morale, their lives,
In capricious weather, on unforgiving
Terrain, taking vague direction and
Ambiguous information
Then persuading, cajoling them, counter
To their own comfort and safety,
To risk injury and death in the name
Of some greater good neither you, nor they
Drafted nor necessarily subscribed
To—and succeeding.

Your record speaks for itself.
You're not actually qualified to do anything.

In Corpore Sano

With such a round, scrubbed face and soft body,
You might be tempted to kick him.
Someone has. But his eyes shine with mischief
In spite of the blue-black bruises underneath.

He stands near the riverbank, there being
Nowhere clean enough for him to sit.
"The street is no place for a germophobe."
He laughs and picks imaginary lint
From the book bag slung over his shoulder.

His scruffy companions chuckle, too.
Perhaps they have heard this before,
After the last beating he took.
They pretend not to notice the slight
When he moves away from them.
To distance himself from ignorance,
He backs into the water's edge
And loses a shoe in the muck.

Startled, he looks from side to side
For somewhere else to be,
Until his shoulders fall, recognizing
That you know what he knows:
He deserves the beatings
For the self he has become,
One with the very dirt he fears.

THE EYE OF THE NEEDLE

He buckles under the weight
Of his wheeled foot locker, as if he were
A porter heading up the gangway
With some *bon vivant*'s travel bar.

But this is all he owns.
And it nearly crushes him.

A sleeping bag, field stove, lawn chair,
Tent, and extra socks drape the surface.
The light rain thwarts his bid to dry them out.
Inside remains a mystery.

The wheels of his *impedimenta*
Have lodged against the crease
In the levee trail, where it rises again
After dipping briefly to pass under the bridge.

The way is not narrow, but steep.

He strains to free himself.
But here he toils in vain,
Unable to move on,
And unable to let go
Without being flattened
Beneath the mass of his estate.

Mad Carl's Neighbors

They lie in wait until certain he is alone.
Then at once they send the floor
Shuddering beneath his feet—
Rumbling under one leg, then the other,
Less pain than nuisance, just to show they own him.

They even drilled tiny holes to watch him eat.
A kitchen wall blotched with putty
Testifies to their inquisitiveness.

They would spy on his sleep if he let them.
But he never sleeps. Sometimes they make love—
So quietly he strains, but can't quite make out
The words through the papery walls.
When he leaves his room in disgust
At two in the morning, he can nearly hear
Their muffled laughs of triumph.

It's not the pipes, or the ductwork,
Or the creaking timbers.
This is deliberate and willful.
Once, he begged them to stop,
But they feigned ignorance, as if confused.

In desperation, he summoned the police,
And the squad car came,
But when the cop knocked on their door,
They lay silent in the darkness
Until he gave up and left.

Carl thought he had learned to cope
With their cruel torment—until
That young girl began snapping her gum.
Now it starts without notice, then stops again:
Click, click, click.

It even happened while I was there,
Waiting with Carl, having sneaked up the back stairwell
To avoid their detection. We sat
Facing each other across the room,
Silent and patient, like anglers waiting for a strike,
Until at last he leaped up, and stabbed at the air.
There! he cried. *Can you hear it? Can you hear it?*
He grinned wildly as his eyes welled with ache
For just one affirming nod.

SKID ROAD

When he is cold and sleeping on the street
because she won't forgive him anymore,
a man can never have too much to eat.

Though other appetites that made him cheat
on her still burn, he dreams of breakfast more
when he is cold and sleeping. On the street,

two shots resolve a life. Check the piece, seat
the clip, and move. Contentment is the whore
a man can never have. Too much to eat

could make him soft. He misses meals to beat
back harder pain, his gut an open sore
when he is cold. And sleeping on the street

comes bitter to him, who once knew what sweet
was. When he finds what he is living for,
a man can never have too much. To eat

then would be sin. But now, his clumsy feet
trip on a rind. He picks it from the floor.
When he is cold and sleeping on the street
a man can never have too much to eat.

LULLABY BENEATH THE BRIDGE

Your nuncle-fury spent, find sleep Old Man,
Before the world begins to stir awake.
The storms that kept you on your feet have passed
And left a cold, familiar disregard,
Receded into workday weariness,
The realm of other souls' torment and grief.

Now, rest beneath these brutal concrete spans
With ramparts built of shopping carts to gird
Your makeshift battlement. Wring out your socks,
And pull your blanket to your hoary chin.

I pray that early walkers won't disturb
This stillness, and that pillars shield your eyes
From the harsh glare of morning's rising sun;
That foolish fears make room for cordial dreams
Of softer beds, and more forgiving bones,
And daughter, striving still to bring you home.

The Man in Flames

He stopped for the Man in Flames
Waving frantically beside the road.
Other drivers looked, out of curiosity,
And continued on. But even though
He would be late for dinner,
He pulled over and got out of his car.

He heard a wail from within
The blaze begging him for help.
So he wrapped the Man in his coat,
And together, they rolled on the ground.

As they lay smoldering in the dirt,
He asked the charred face what had happened.
"I tried to kill myself," the Man said,
"Then I changed my mind. Am I going to die?"
Not yet, he said.

He got home late. Neither the paramedics,
Nor the police, nor his wife
Believed his story.

Three days later, he read in the paper
The Man in Flames had died.
On his way home from work that night,
He stopped for a drink. He didn't say anything
When his wife asked him why.

When a Man sets himself on fire,

If he doesn't die of shock or infection,

He will most likely die from dehydration.

Without his skin, he is lost.

And even if you put out the fire,

You can never be sure

That you did the right thing,

Or whether events, once in motion,

Should have stayed that way.

The Traveler Addresses the Good Samaritan

We know one another, don't we?
Not socially, of course. Merely in passing,
As I was once fully capable of caring for myself,
So you couldn't have been bothered.

But as I came and went,
I felt you watching me, patiently
Marking time until I slipped into the ditch,
Either on my own or (as I began to suspect)
With help.

You must thank God
For roving bands of robbers,
Without whom you would be
Just another meddling pariah,
Always ready to set aside
Your own responsibilities
To offer succor and advice
To those who never asked for either.

Now you dictate what I wear, and eat,
And where I lay my head.
And no doubt you will make it known
What you have done for my sake.
I can't stop you.

Just don't say that I was grateful.
Others will assume what they will,

But perhaps someday,
A kindred spirit will read between the lines
And find another lesson altogether:

Help is just another form of control.

CRAB LICE

Crab lice—Crab lice!
   I lost my sense—
Crab lice is now
   The consequence!

Surrender—all thought—
   Of amorous arts—
Start putting lotion
   On nether parts!

And change out—the locks—
   Ah—I'm free!
At last from a—parasite—
   Like thee!

... and He is Us

INQUISITION

Everyone needs a good inquisition
Now and then. The converted
Will discover they have something
For which to live; and the persecuted,
Something for which to die.

ATTACK OF THE BLUE TARP ZOMBIES

They keep coming closer and closer,
Smothering the landscape in their sea
Of Smurf-blue polyethylene. They first take hold
In the countryside, where they feast
On entropy and expediency. Eventually
They insinuate themselves into sheds,
Garages, back yards, and rooftops.
They settle everywhere, and for good enough.
Before you can react, they will have you surrounded:

Paint-splattered drop cloth, rain fly,
Ground cloth, tent, wood pile cover,
Inoperable or superfluous
Boat, car, trailer, bike, and tractor cover,
Helicopter landing zone marker,
Wind sock, sail, gardening hot house,
Poncho, kite and tail, roof patch, wall patch,
Awning, window blind, pond liner,
Luggage-loaded roof rack cover,
Table cloth, picnic blanket, sofa slip cover,
Sign, and flag. They are relentless.

You can't hunt them down because
You can't tell friend from foe.
They could be you, or me,
Except that they are color-blind
And deaf to their grumbling neighbors.
Even now, just across the street,

There is what appears to be a man
Offering to lend you one to cover
Your barbecue grill. He says it looks like rain.
Go ahead. Take it. It's only for a while.

"Premise Under Surveillance"
(signs in a corporate parking lot)

Our executives at last realize
That careless thinking poses a greater threat
To corporate health than double parking.
And we may enter with impunity
Into the tawdriest of backseat encounters
So long as we avoid sloppiness
In our major and minor propositions.

But just which premise are they watching?
And why not the whole syllogism?
Careful, my friend.
Form even your most private thoughts
With rigor and precision.
Be certain conclusions follow from assertions.

All across the corporate campus,
Curbside, under street lamps,
Mid-level staffers plead for leniency
From logicians and philosophy majors on patrol:
"But Officer, that was an enthymeme;
The supposition was implied!"

ECO-TERRORISM LITE

Plastic bottles and aluminum cans
Stacked defiantly atop
The single trash receptacle in the break area:
A most civil disobedience.

ALL HALLOW'S EVE AT STARBUCKS

Supergirl stands with her hand on her hip.
Her blue cape rests against her elbow
As she waits for her usual
Tall soy latte, extra foam.

Meanwhile, outside, the mayhem
Continues unchecked. Those
Intent on mischief rove from
Door to door with impunity.
Supergirl remains serenely oblivious.
She twists slightly on her red high heels
To show off her calves,
Now that she has freed them for the evening
From her knee-capping boots.

She takes her order and waves
To the barista as she wends
Through the pack of monsters
Still waiting for their turn.
Pikachu stops on his way in
To hold the door for her.
She smiles, nods in recognition
And takes another sip as she
Steps back into the dark night.

THE CHURCH OF FOOTBALL

The Church of Football baptizes in blood.
  It oozes, like Velveeta through corn chips,
  Then clots in cleats like over-baked bean dips.
Why does this spectacle make men crave food?
Backs fight for yards through mud, with mud, in mud;
  While fervent fans use sleeves to lave their lips
And relish each hard hit between their sips
Of beer, which wash down a bacon-lade spud.

Yet for all this, there still is room for more;
  The fantasy league player, safe from stings
Of gladiatorial combat, or
  The stress of standing for the anthem, brings
All appetites to bear, devouring gore
  With plates of warm brats and with ah! hot wings.

BELLY BUMPING

Reared up, prick-eared
At some imagined transgression;
Backs arched, distended solar plexuses
Weighing on the belt lines
Cinched with leather, chrome, and brass;
Circling warily
Through the thicket of three-axis routers,
Cutting tables, autoclaves,
Band saws and hot-form presses;
But hands empty,
Dropped loosely to their sides:
This is not a death match;
Just two of the afflicted
Careening roly-poly off one another's guts
In defense of their patches of concrete—
Marked by rolling tool boxes
And scattered *Hot Rod* magazines—
Against insult, usurpation, and disrespect,
And all so they can pay
To send their daughters
Off to soccer camp.

ROAD CREW BABE

Does a union wage or guilty pleasure drive you
To pose for every gawking passerby?
You lift your hand, and gladly we obey.
But before you catch me scrutinizing legs,
And tan,
And bust,
I feign attention to my rearview mirror
And see the man behind me look away
In our mutual dance of awkward nonchalance,
An unsteady dissolution of our lust and fear.
Underneath the hard hat, your bleached hair glistens
Like asphalt, freshly laid,
Curing in the evening sun.
And the homemade tattoo on your trapezius
Suggests you are no stranger to boredom
Or to pain. There is little doubt
That you have seen and heard
Whatever I can imagine: smoking,
Drinking, cursing, sweating
With the worst of us. I never see
The likes of your creased face
And yellow, wolf eyes in my cul-de-sac.
And yet, for all your cock-hipped posturing,
You and I both know you offer only two speeds:
Stop. And Slow.

THE GOOD WORD MISSION CHURCH IN THE STRIP MALL

Save your soul today.

Save ten per cent on oil changes

With minimum contribution.

Payday loans available next door.

Nails done while you wait.

Ample parking.

Open Sundays.

POVERTY BAY

At sunset's high tide, the waves slap
Against the concrete bulkhead
And rebound upwards, foam splashing
Between the boardwalk's broad planks.
A woman crouches behind a lamppost
And wrings the neck
Of an unsuspecting drake.
Her dog shakes salt water from its belly
As its mistress turns for home
Its toenails clicking along the slats
While it hurries to keep pace,
Goaded by the fretful cries
Of gulls overhead.

COOKING SHOW

Watch carefully as I combine a tablespoon
(you don't have that?)
and two teaspoons
(it only seems expensive)
with three cups
(the brand is key, though I doubt this one
is available where you live),
add water, and stir constantly
for more time than you can spare,
maintaining a uniform viscosity
with this precision instrument,
which you can build at home
(feel free to send for the plans).

It will look so much more seductive
if you serve it in one of these
(though I suppose you will have to make do
with whatever you happen to own).
If you had friends with highly cultivated sensibilities,
they would agree with me
that this is both delicious and beautiful,
and they would defer to you
in matters of taste and discernment,
but until next week, I can only hope
that you enjoyed as much as I
the hour we have spent imagining
the life you'll never have.

GREAT BOOKS OF THE WESTERN WORLD

There are only so many times you can re-read Aquinas.
Or so I'm told. Still, you could. If you choose.
David Foster Wallace did, for as long as he could bear it.

And to have done so until you are weary of him—
His jokes worn thin (you must have heard the one
About truth, wine, the king, and woman),
His syllogisms stale, his niceties of the knower
And the known, all that straining to cling
To a thread of optimism in an imperfect happiness—
May leave you destitute, or mad, or both.

"There are only so many times you can re-read Aquinas,"
She shrugged, pulling back her headset
Just long enough to count the money
And surrender the well-thumbed volumes,
Inured to the stench of cat urine,
To the boxes cluttered around her,
To life outside her single-wide, even to the tedium
That paid her rent and put bread on her table.
Then she adjusted her headset and took the next call.

"English, Please"

She understands the question,
But her eyes frantically search the room
For the words to answer,
As if looking for a missing set of keys.
Of course she knows.
She knows Pushkin's "Angel,"
Breughel's "Icarus," and Chopin's
"Prelude Number Four." But these
And the treasures of her mother tongue
Are lost to her now,
Fallen down the cracks
Between the language of comfort
And the language of commerce.
So she winces as she answers haltingly,
And with each syllable
The vision of her past thins
Like a silhouette on the horizon
And each promise of the future
Must be paid for in the hard currency
Of "English, please."

Trinity Row House Brickwork

Trace the crooked mortar with your finger
Along its uneven courses
And you encounter other fingers on your way
Embedded in the misshapen bricks—

Smaller fingers, the hand prints of children
Who must have quickly ceased
To see the game in it all,
Making mud pies to earn their daily bread.

Were they beaten for their carelessness?
Were they pushed to work faster,
Knowing that whatever they created
Was good enough for the likes of these?

Why should their masters care
This work might one day show
In walls stripped of their plaster
And expose these tiny hands
Again reaching through the clay?

MANHATTAN

A pushy martini,
Vermouth in coarser company,
At once overly cloying
And excessively bitter,
A dark assault on the senses,
Leaving no room for grace or subtlety.
Impatience with a cherry on top.

WASPS

"Kill them if you have to.
I just don't want them here."
She was accustomed to deciding
What stays, what lives.
A volunteer Michaelmas daisy
Without a sense of proportion
Would not last long. Nor would the wasps.

"There!" she said. A lone *vespula vulgaris*
Had emerged from a narrow slit
Beneath the far pillar of the portico,
Somersaulted in the air, and set out
To forage for food. For a time,
It had found sanctuary here,
But when she decided to place the trellis
For a climbing *rosa floribunda* nearby,
This wasp became superfluous,
And now they all must die.

At sunset, in twos and threes,
The wasps returned to their colony,
Having feasted on caterpillars and flies,
And needing rest and protection
In the failing light. It was not to be.
Meanwhile the bumble bees meandered,
Unmolested among the lavender,
And the foxglove stalks swayed in the breeze,
Well upwind from the toxins

That sent the wasps confused and staggering

Out from beneath the pillar,

Desperate for air, and life,

And finding neither.

Annual Performance Review

If it were up to me, we wouldn't
Even be having this conversation.
I have never understood
How facing your shortcomings
Head-on has engendered anything but grief.

You and I both know you could do better,
So why belabor the point?

You take what you get,
Do the best you can with it,
And hope no one notices
Before you move on.

You know I'd like to give you more this year—
And I'm sure it's little consolation
That I didn't fare much better.
Yes, I could have asked for more,
But really, I couldn't see the point.

Perhaps I lack a certain kind of courage.
Well, all right, I do. I am a coward.

And I assumed (wrongly, it seems)
You would sit there and take it
With the rest of us.
We can all learn something from this I suppose
What I mean to say is—Please!
For God's sake, don't shoot!

About Fomite

A fomite is a medium capable of transmitting infectious organisms from one individual to another.

"The activity of art is based on the capacity of people to be infected by the feelings of others." Tolstoy, *What Is Art?*

Writing a review on Amazon, Good Reads, Shelfari, Library Thing or other social media sites for readers will help the progress of independent publishing. To submit a review, go to the book page on any of the sites and follow the links for reviews. Books from independent presses rely on reader to reader communications.

For more information or to order any of our books, visit
http://www.fomitepress.com/FOMITE/Our_Books.html

More Titles from Fomite...

Novels

Lamar Herrin — *Father Figure*
Michael Horner — *Damage Control*
Ron Jacobs — *All the Sinners Saints*
Ron Jacobs — *Short Order Frame Up*
Ron Jacobs — *The Co-conspirator's Tale*
Scott Archer Jones — *And Throw Away the Skins*
Scott Archer Jones — *A Rising Tide of People Swept Away*
Julie Justicz — *Degrees of Difficulty*
Maggie Kast — *A Free Unsullied Land*
Darrell Kastin — *Shadowboxing with Bukowski*
Coleen Kearon — *#triggerwarning*
Coleen Kearon — *Feminist on Fire*
Jan English Leary — *Thicker Than Blood*
Diane Lefer — *Confessions of a Carnivore*
Rob Lenihan — *Born Speaking Lies*
Douglas Milliken — *Our Shadow's Voice*
Colin Mitchell — *Roadman*
Ilan Mochari — *Zinsky the Obscure*
Peter Nash — *Parsimony*
Peter Nash — *The Perfection of Things*
George Ovitt — *Stillpoint*
George Ovitt — *Tribunal*
Gregory Papadoyiannis — *The Baby Jazz*
Pelham — *The Walking Poor*
Andy Potok — *My Father's Keeper*
Frederick Ramey — *Comes A Time*
Joseph Rathgeber — *Mixedbloods*
Kathryn Roberts — *Companion Plants*
Robert Rosenberg — *Isles of the Blind*
Fred Russell — *Rafi's World*
Ron Savage — *Voyeur in Tangier*
David Schein — *The Adoption*
Lynn Sloan — *Principles of Navigation*
L.E. Smith — *The Consequence of Gesture*
L.E. Smith — *Travers' Inferno*
L.E. Smith — *Untimely RIPped*
Bob Sommer — *A Great Fullness*
Tom Walker — *A Day in the Life*
Susan V. Weiss — *My God, What Have We Done?*
Peter M. Wheelwright — *As It Is On Earth*
Suzie Wizowaty — *The Return of Jason Green*

Poetry

Scott T. Starbuck — *Hawk on Wire*
Scott T. Starbuck — *Industrial Oz*
Seth Steinz r — *Among the Lost*
Seth Steinzor — *To Join the Lost*
Susan Thomas — *In the Sadness Museum*
Susan Thomas — *The Empty Notebook Interrogates Itself*
Paolo Valesio/Todd Portnowitz — *La Mezzanotte di Spoleto/Midnight in Spoleto*
Sharon Webster — *Everyone Lives Here*
Tony Whedon — *The Tres Riches Heures*
Tony Whedon — *The Falkland Quartet*
Claire Zoghb — *Dispatches from Everest*

Stories
Jay Boyer — *Flight*
L. M Brown — *Treading the Uneven Road*
Michael Cocchiarale — *Here Is Ware*
Michael Cocchiarale — *Still Time*
Neil Connelly — *In the Wake of Our Vows*
Catherine Zobal Dent — *Unfinished Stories of Girls*
Zdravka Evtimova —*Carts and Other Stories*
John Michael Flynn — *Off to the Next Wherever*
Derek Furr — *Semitones*
Derek Furr — *Suite for Three Voices*
Elizabeth Genovise — *Where There Are Two or More*
Andrei Guriuanu — *Body of Work*
Zeke Jarvis — *In A Family Way*
Arya Jenkins — *Blue Songs in an Open Key*
Jan English Leary — *Skating on the Vertical*
Marjorie Maddox — *What She Was Saying*
William Marquess — *Boom-shacka-lacka*
Gary Miller — *Museum of the Americas*
Jennifer Anne Moses — *Visiting Hours*
Martin Ott — *Interrogations*
Christopher Peterson — *Amoebic Simulacra*
Jack Pulaski — *Love's Labours*
Charles Rafferty — *Saturday Night at Magellan's*
Ron Savage — *What We Do For Love*
Fred Skolnik— *Americans and Other Stories*
Lynn Sloan — *This Far Is Not Far Enough*
L.E. Smith — *Views Cost Extra*
Caitlin Hamilton Summie — *To Lay To Rest Our Ghosts*

Made in the USA
San Bernardino, CA
05 March 2019